W9-DED-497

# ABDO
## Publishing Company

# Keep Clean

GET HEALTHY

Buddy BOOKS
Get Healthy

A Buddy Book by **Sarah Tieck**

## VISIT US AT
### www.abdopublishing.com

Published by ABDO Publishing Company, PO Box 398166, Minneapolis, MN 55439.

Copyright © 2012 by Abdo Consulting Group, Inc. International copyrights reserved in all countries. No part of this book may be reproduced in any form without written permission from the publisher. Buddy Books™ is a trademark and logo of ABDO Publishing Company.

Printed in the United States of America, North Mankato, Minnesota.
102011
012012

 PRINTED ON RECYCLED PAPER

Coordinating Series Editor: Rochelle Baltzer
Contributing Editors: Megan M. Gunderson, BreAnn Rumsch, Marcia Zappa
Graphic Design: Jenny Christensen
Cover Photograph: *iStockphoto*: ©iStockphoto.com/EMPPhotography.
Interior Photographs/Illustrations: *Eighth Street Studio* (p. 26); *Glow Images*: ©Ariel Skelley/CORBIS (p. 5); *iStockphoto*: ©iStockphoto.com/CEFutcher (p. 7), ©iStockphoto.com/Figure8Photos (p. 21), ©iStockphoto.com/JenniferPhotographyImaging (p. 13), ©iStockphoto.com/kati1313 (p. 27), ©iStockphoto.com/michellegibson (p. 26), ©iStockphoto.com/sefaoncul (p. 29), ©iStockphoto.com/somethingway (p. 15), ©iStockphoto.com/the4js (p. 30), ©iStockphoto.com/timsa (p. 25); *Shutterstock*: Cheryl Casey (p. 17), Lilya Espinosa (p. 9), Fine Shine (p. 27) Firma V (p. 11), GeoM (p. 19), MANDY GODBEHEAR (p. 23), Kamira (p. 11), Morgan Lane Photography (p. 30), StockLite (p. 19), Zurijeta (p. 17).

### Library of Congress Cataloging-in-Publication Data

Tieck, Sarah, 1976-
  Keep clean / Sarah Tieck.
     p. cm. -- (Get healthy)
  ISBN 978-1-61783-234-5
  1. Hygiene--Juvenile literature. I. Title.
  RA780.T54 2012
  613--dc23
                          2011034603

# Table of Contents

Healthy Living ................................ 4

Clean Up ...................................... 6

Fresh and Clean ............................. 10

Clean Hands ................................. 12

Shiny Teeth ................................. 14

Clothes Smart ............................... 18

Clean Spaces ................................ 20

Now and Later ............................... 22

Brain Food .................................. 26

Making Healthy Choices ...................... 28

Healthy Body Files .......................... 30

Important Words ............................. 31

Web Sites ................................... 31

Index ....................................... 32

# Healthy Living

Your body is amazing! It does thousands of things each day. It lets you jump, smell, and play. A healthy body helps you feel good and live well!

In order to be healthy, you must take care of your body. One way to do this is to keep clean. So, let's learn more about **hygiene** and neatness!

Good hygiene helps people look, smell, and feel their best.

# Clean Up

Good personal **hygiene** means caring for your body and appearance. Messy hair and dirty clothes may not seem like a problem. But, keeping clean makes you feel good. And, it can **protect** you from sickness.

Your appearance is one of the first things people notice about you. So, take care of your clothes, hair, and body!

When a person has poor **hygiene**, their body and clothes may smell or look messy. Dirt, sweat, oil, and dead skin cells collect on them.

Poor hygiene may also make people sick. Dirty hands can spread **germs**. Always wash your hands after using the bathroom. Also wash up if you cough or sneeze into your hand.

Make sure you dry off properly after bathing.
Some types of germs grow on wet skin.

# Fresh and Clean

Bathing regularly is important. Doing this removes dirt and **germs** that collect on your skin.

You can take showers or baths to get clean. Wash your body using soap and warm water. Wash your hair with shampoo.

WORD OF MOUTH

If your hair isn't clean, it might look oily.

Comb your hair to help it appear neat. But, be sure to use your own comb. This prevents the spread of lice.

# Clean Hands

Your hands touch many things during the day. You use them when you open doors, throw away trash, and eat food. Because your hands touch so many things, you need to wash them often.

Don't forget about your fingernails! **Germs** can hide under them. So, clean them when you wash your hands and trim them regularly.

WORD OF MOUTH

Be sure to wash your hands properly. Make soap suds and then scrub your skin for at least 20 seconds.

If you help cook meals, wash your hands before and after. Certain foods, such as raw meat, can make you sick. And if you cook with dirty hands, you can spread germs.

# Shiny Teeth

Brushing your teeth is part of good **hygiene**. If you don't brush enough, a type of **bacteria** called plaque builds up on teeth. This can cause a **cavity**.

Brush your teeth with toothpaste at least twice a day. Most people brush in the morning and at night. Brushing after each meal is even better. This gets food off teeth right away.

**How It Sounds**

plaque (PLAK)

Brush the top, bottom, front, and back sides of your teeth. Don't forget to brush your tongue!

Change your toothbrush every three to four months. Also, do this after you have been sick. And, never share your toothbrush.

WORD OF MOUTH

Sometimes after eating, food gets stuck between teeth. So in addition to brushing, you need to floss. This will remove food pieces stuck between your teeth.

Visiting a dentist regularly can prevent many tooth problems. Dentists give your teeth a deep cleaning. They check the health and growth of your teeth. And, they can treat any problems.

Dentists use special tools to deep clean your teeth.

Flossing helps keep your gums healthy. Gently slide the floss in and curve it around your teeth.

WORD OF MOUTH

Sugary drinks and candy cause cavities. So, enjoy these only once in a while!

# Clothes Smart

When your body and teeth are clean, put on a clean outfit. This includes underwear, socks, and clothes.

Most of the time you only need one outfit each day. But if you get dirty, change into clean clothes. Set aside your dirty clothes to be washed. Washing clothes removes dead skin and **bacteria**.

Smelly, dirty clothes are not usually unhealthy. But, they may bother you and those around you.

The best way to keep your room clean is to make it a habit. That means you clean it regularly, such as every day or every week.

# Clean Spaces

Keeping your room and school desk neat is also part of being clean. It is easier to stay healthy when your space is clean. Dusty, dirty spaces make some people cough and sneeze!

At home, make your bed each day. Put away toys, books, and clothes. At school, keep your desk tidy. Put away books, notebooks, crayons, and glue. When a space is neat, wipe it clean.

Mice, bugs, and dust are often found in dirty spaces. These can make people sick.

# Now and Later

Good **hygiene** helps you feel good about yourself. And, it will help people want to spend more time with you.

Keeping your space clean is also important. This can help you be on time and study well. When your space is tidy, you can find things and stay focused more easily!

You are around other people at home, at school, and someday at work. So, good hygiene is important.

Besides helping you look and feel good, proper **hygiene protects** your body. **Bacteria** can make you sick or cause **cavities** in your teeth.

Some bacteria can lead to serious problems, such as heart trouble. Make good choices now to keep your body healthy for many years!

Boogers have an important job. They trap germs before they enter your body. Picking your nose puts those germs on your hands. So, don't pick!

WORD OF MOUTH

When you sneeze, cover your nose and mouth with your arm. That way, germs don't spread as far.

# Brain Food

## How often do I need to wash my hands?

Even if your hands don't look dirty, they may have germs on them! So, wash them before you cook or eat. Wash them if you will be holding a baby. And wash them after you go to the bathroom, blow your nose, touch animals, or play outside.

# How long do I need to brush my teeth?

Many dentists suggest brushing for two minutes. Some people use a clock to make sure they brush long enough.

# Why do people wear deodorant?

As you get older, your body sweats more. When sweat combines with skin **bacteria**, it can smell bad. So, adults and some kids put deodorant on their underarms. This helps them smell better!

# Making Healthy Choices

Remember that keeping clean keeps you healthy! So, learn some daily habits. By caring for your body every day, you will help your health.

**Hygiene** is just one part of a healthy life. Each positive choice you make will help you stay healthy!

Hand washing is a simple but powerful tool to help you stay healthy. Sing "Happy Birthday" two times in your head to make sure you wash long enough!

## CLEAN UP

✔ When you go to the bathroom, your body lets out liquid and solid waste. So, wipe to remove any left on your body. Then, wash your hands.

✔ Wear clean underwear every day.

## TOOTH LOVE

✔ Eating calcium-rich foods keeps your teeth healthy and strong. These foods include milk, cheese, and yogurt.

✔ Braces make it harder to clean bacteria off your teeth. So if you have them, take extra care when brushing and flossing.

## TOE JAM

✔ Lots of skin bacteria collects between your toes. So, spend extra time cleaning off the toe jam!

# Important Words

**bacteria** (bak-TIHR-ee-uh) tiny, one-celled organisms that can only be seen through a microscope. Some are germs.

**cavity** a rotten or sick part of a tooth.

**germs** (JUHRMS) harmful organisms that can make people sick.

**hygiene** (HEYE-jeen) practices done to keep the body clean and healthy.

**protect** (pruh-TEHKT) to guard against harm or danger.

# Web Sites

To learn more about keeping clean, visit ABDO Publishing Company online. Web sites about keeping clean are featured on our Book Links page. These links are routinely monitored and updated to provide the most current information available.

## www.abdopublishing.com

# Index

bacteria **14, 18, 24, 27, 30**

body **4, 6, 7, 8, 10, 18, 24, 27, 28, 30**

cavities **14, 17, 24**

clothes **6, 7, 8, 18, 19, 20, 30**

dentists **16, 17, 27**

floss **16, 17, 30**

germs **8, 9, 10, 12, 13, 24, 25, 26**

gums **17**

hair **6, 7, 10, 11**

hands **8, 12, 13, 24, 26, 29, 30**

nails **12**

shampoo **10**

sicknesses **6, 8, 13, 15, 21, 24**

skin **8, 9, 10, 12, 18, 27, 30**

soap **10, 12**

spaces **20, 21, 22**

sweat **8, 27**

teeth **14, 15, 16, 17, 18, 24, 27, 30**

toothbrush **15**

toothpaste **14**